Cà d'Zan

THE RESTORATION OF
THE RINGLING MANSION

MICHELLE A. SCALERA

EDITED BY DEBORAH W. WALK

This publication was made possible through generous support from
Florida Department of State, Bureau of Historic Preservation,
Division of Historical Resources, Community Education Grant and
Michael Saunders & Company

Printing and Separations by Serbin Printing & Publishing, Inc., Sarasota, Florida
Robin K. Clark, Project Director
Judy Webster, Designer
Jim Keen, Production Manager

All new photography by Giovanni Lunardi Photography, Sarasota, Florida,
unless otherwise noted.

All historic photographs from the Museum Archives, unless otherwise noted.

Copyright 2006 © The John and Mable Ringling Museum of Art
The State Art Museum of Florida
5401 Bay Shore Road
Sarasota, Florida 34243
www.ringling.org

PUBLISHER'S CATALOGING–IN–PUBLICATION DATA
Scalera, Michelle A.
72 p.: ill.; 24 cm.
Introduction: John Wetenhall, Paul Miller.
1. Cà d'Zan (Sarasota, Fla.) 2. Eclecticism in architecture–Florida–Sarasota
3. Architecture–Florida–Sarasota–20th century.
4. Mansions–Conservation and restoration–Florida– Sarasota.
5. Sarasota (Fla.)–Buildings, structures, etc.
6. Ringling, John, 1866–1936–Homes and haunts–Florida–Sarasota.
7. Ringling Mable, 1875–1929–Homes and haunts–Florida–Sarasota.
I. Miller, Paul. II. The John and Mable Ringling Museum of Art.

NA7511.4 .S27 S43 2006   ISBN 9780916758530

Library of Congress Control Number: 2006934152

Front Cover: *Dancers of the Nations* by Willy Pogany

The John and Mable
RINGLING
Museum of Art
THE STATE ART MUSEUM OF FLORIDA
FLORIDA STATE UNIVERSITY

The John and Mable Ringling Museum of Art
Dr. John Wetenhall, Executive Director

Florida State University
Dr. Thomas Kent "T.K." Wetherell, President

⚬⚬⚬⚬⚬⚬
CONTENTS

iv   EXECUTIVE DIRECTOR'S WELCOME

     INTRODUCTION

     PREFACE

1   CÀ D'ZAN – JOHN AND MABLE RINGLING'S SEASONAL RESIDENCE

3   BUILDING AND PEOPLE

5   MASS AND MATERIALS

8   HISTORY OF CONSERVATION EFFORTS

9   PHASED CONSTRUCTION PROJECTS

       Phase I   12

       Phase II   19

       Phase III   27

       Second Floor   47

       Third Floor   57

       Fourth Floor   58

61   CONCLUSION – CÀ D'ZAN RETURNED TO SPLENDOR

62   APPENDICES

       Floor Plan Layout   62

       Donors to the Restoration Project   63

       Cà d'Zan Facts   63

       Companies and Professionals   64

66   BIBLIOGRAPHY

EXECUTIVE DIRECTOR'S WELCOME

Moviegoers across America came to know John Ringling's epic Venetian mansion, "Cà d'Zan," with the 1998 release of the film, *Great Expectations*, starring Gwyneth Paltrow, Ethan Hawke, and featuring Anne Bancroft as the modern-day personification of Dickens' famous character, Miss Havisham. Little make-up was required for creating the ruin of the Havisham residence. Cà d'Zan, through years of deferred maintenance and outright neglect had already fallen into disrepair. Buffeted by salt-sea winds and waves, the stonework had deteriorated, making Cà d'Zan's lavish marble terrace a danger to visitors. The old system of climate controls – open windows – had caused walls and fabrics to fade. Mechanical systems ground to a halt.

By the mid 1990's, the sad condition of John and Mable Ringling's once glorious showplace caused the local community to take action. Appeals were made to state legislators to save its mansion, the Ringling being officially recognized as "The State Art Museum of Florida." Funding appeals went out and, through a combination of sources – public and private; local, state and national – funds were raised to restore Sarasota's architectural treasure. A six-year campaign began in 1996 that would lead to three phases of its ultimate restoration. Once again one of America's Castles, the mansion reopened to a grateful and adoring public in April of 2002.

The pages that follow will tell you about the processes that led to the mansion's revival, the collaboration among architects, conservators, curators, contractors, and public officials that restored the Ringling mansion back to its former life. We must acknowledge the significant contributions from Florida's Department of State, its Division of Historical Resources, and its Bureau of Historic Preservation, as well as many private foundations and individuals who contributed the funds necessary to complete the restoration. In 2000, governance of the Ringling Museum was transferred to Florida State University, which saw to the project's timely and fiscally sound completion. In the end, it cost over $15 million – a tribute to the passion and love that local and state leadership devoted to its part of Ringling history. But as a cautionary tale, such a project should have required only a fraction of those millions, had caring and forward-looking maintenance been administered all along.

John Wetenhall, Ph.D. , *Executive Director*

INTRODUCTION

"We should comport ourselves with the masterpieces of art as with exalted personages – stand quietly before them and wait till they speak to us."
Arthur Schopenhauer, German, 1788–1860

It has been a long wait for those seeking to draw some words of revelation from John and Mable Ringling's highly personalized masterpiece of art, their distinctive Sarasota winter home, Cà d'Zan. Even more than William Randolph Hearst's otherworldly mountaintop lair at San Simeon, or the opulent stage sets of the Newport Gilded Age "cottages," Cà d'Zan was marked with the imprint of its builders' impassioned vision. But as years passed, finishes grew tarnished, the placement of objects was changed, temporary repairs became permanent and the structural and decorative fabric of the seaside retreat was compromised.

John Ringling, the humbly born circus entrepreneur, manifested a lifelong ambition to become one of America's exalted personages and to live like one in a setting conveying wealth and informed taste. He wished to speak to future generations, standing reverently before his built legacy, of a boy from Iowa's rise to success, of his personal fulfillment in becoming an architectural patron and in the active burst of his serious art collecting. In other words, Ringling wished to speak to us of the American Dream. That voice dimmed considerably over time. Today, however, after six years of exhaustive research, conservation and restoration, John and Mable Ringling's legacy stands renewed and revealed, the interplay of its design elements rebalanced, the signature of the Ringlings all the more legible. We no longer have to wait to discern a message, John Ringling's voice speaks clearly and distinctly and Cà d'Zan echoes his words, it is the museum of the American Dream.

Paul Miller, *Curator,*
The Preservation Society of Newport County

PREFACE

Cà d'Zan "so riotously, exuberantly gorgeously
fantastic, so far out of the world of normality…"
Henry Ringling North in *The Circus Kings*

The restoration of the Cà d'Zan was the culmination of a multi-year project, which required the support of many individuals who need to be acknowledged for their assistance. First, the Florida Department of State, Division of Historical Resources preservation experts in Tallahassee, Florida, moved the project forward in the early stages and throughout the restoration. I would like to especially thank George Percy, Fred Gaske, Walter Marder, David Ferro, and Robert Taylor, of the Division of Historical Resources for their valuable help. Herschel Sheppard, preservation architect from Gainesville, Florida and Nicholas Pappas, architect from Richmond, Virginia, deserve special thanks for their assistance and for their preliminary reports that initiated the restoration process.

Architects, contractors, construction engineers, carpenters, electricians, directors, curators, archivists, librarians, conservators, restorers, artisans, painters, photographers and many more were all critical to the work in what evolved into a six year, $15 million dollar project. The restoration of Cà d'Zan could not have been possible without generous financial support from State grants, private foundations and donors.

Sincere thanks and appreciation to Teresa Koncick, Deborah Walk, Ron McCarty, David Piurek, and Jennifer Kouvant, for their ongoing support of this project; without them, this publication would not have been possible. I wish to express my thanks to the Museum staff for their assistance: Lynn Berkowitz, Paula Parrish, Larissa Enzmann, Carol Tayman, Suellen Field, Linda McKee, Sherry Rundell, Liz Gray, Jennifer Posey, and Melissa Porreca. My heartfelt thanks is extended to Michael Saunders, who has been essential to the creation of this publication.

Michelle Scalera

CÀ D'ZAN
JOHN AND MABLE RINGLING'S
SEASONAL RESIDENCE

*The remarkable feature of the life of John Ringling was neither
his ability to accumulate wealth nor his egocentrism, but rather the
inner complexity of his personality, formed by nature and experience,
together with a quickness of mind that enabled him to grasp and
assimilate new elements into a life already richly filled."*
Dr. David Weeks, Ringling Historian

The history and splendor of the Ringling mansion is an impressive legacy. Located on a 66-acre estate, the home of John and Mable Ringling, Cà d'Zan, began the path to building their dreams of an ideally situated residence followed by construction of a remarkable art museum for their collections. The home has 41 rooms, 15 baths, 107 operable internal doors, 97 windows, a lower level basement and is over 36,000 square feet; 23,000 square feet under air. The terrace, located on the west façade is 200 feet by 40 feet, and was capable of accommodating John Ringling's 125 foot yacht, the *Zalophus*. The final cost of the construction was $1,500,000 at completion in October 1925. After the interior decorating was completed, the Ringlings welcomed family to their winter residence in December 1926.

John Ringling   Mable Ringling

The circus impresario's winter home, a Venetian *palazzo*, located in a
tropical setting on Sarasota Bay in Florida

1

John Ringling was born in 1866 in McGregor, Iowa, the sixth of seven sons and one daughter. His parents, August and Marie Salomé (Juliar) Ringling were German immigrants. After seeing a riverboat circus in 1869/70, the boys decided upon a circus career. With hard work and dedication, the five Ringling brothers created a circus empire that still exists today. As John Ringling would say later, they "divided the work, but stood together," each managing a part of the family circus.

John Ringling is thought to have met Mable Burton in Chicago and they were married on December 29, 1905, in New Jersey. They sailed together to Europe on a combined honeymoon and business trip. Later, the annual trips included searching for art treasures as well as new circus attractions. One interesting combination, perhaps an example of John Ringling's travels inspiring a circus spectacle, was the "Roman Carnival" Julius Caesar staged for Cleopatra which the Ringling Bros. Circus performance re-enacted as *Caesar's Triumphal Entry into Rome* in 1891. Two Flemish tapestries from a 17th century Caesar series were later purchased by the Ringlings, one was installed in Cà d'Zan, on the mezzanine level directly in front of the Aeolian organ pipes.

Earl Purdy's drawing of Cà d'Zan, ca. 1924

While John Ringling was involved in the construction of the mansion, it was Mable Ringling who was actively engaged in the design of their winter residence. She initially spoke with a Sarasota architect, Thomas R. Martin —whose son Frank created some preliminary drawings, but in the end, Dwight James Baum was selected to create the mansion of their dreams.

BUILDING AND PEOPLE
"Masterful Historic Architect"

Dwight James Baum from Riverdale-on-Hudson, New York, was ultimately the chosen architect for the Ringling mansion. Baum was awarded a Medal of Honor by the Architectural League of New York in 1923 for his "achievements in designing country houses." He designed three Sarasota buildings that are now historic landmarks: Cà d'Zan, the Hotel El Vernona, a 150 room hotel with John Ringling North's "M'Toto" Lounge (now demolished) and the downtown Sarasota County Courthouse.

Baum terra cotta plaque: lost in 21st century

The 1927 oversize book entitled: *The Work of Dwight James Baum Architect* by Matlack Price, documents his numerous architectural residence designs. In the chapter "The Italian Type" Price states, "granted that all Italian houses in this country are radical adaptations." Baum received an award from the American Institute of Architects (AIA) for designing "the best two-story house…1926–30 in America." This was the Francis Collins home No 4521 Delafield Avenue, dated 1925–26 in the Fieldston area of New York.

The Ringling mansion, Cà d'Zan, was cited and mentioned, yet not illustrated in the publication: "Mr. Baum has recently designed a number of buildings in the Spanish manner for the West Coast of Florida…They constitute an interesting and timely expression of his work." It may be that the book went to press prior to Baum receiving the photographs taken by Samuel H. Gottscho.

In January 2006, a comprehensive research project was presented to the New York City Landmarks Preservation Commission, (NYLPC) on the Fieldston region of Riverdale, New York residences. The NYLPC designated the suburban community as the Fieldston Historic District, initiated as land purchased in 1829 by Joseph Delafield. Over 62 existing buildings of the 257 architect designed houses are being cited as contributing properties. Remarkably Baum designed 140 buildings within the catalog of all the residences. Anthony Robins, former Director of Surveys for the Landmark Preservation Commission has written numerous articles and provided supportive research. The 449-page report provides exhaustive historical, archival and photographic documentation asserting the overwhelming number of architecturally diverse properties Baum so capably constructed in a relatively short period of time. Baum's Fieldston work spans the period from 1914–1939 with a broad range of styles including Tudor, Greek Revival, Mediterranean Revival, Colonial and Georgian designs.

Owen Burns, a Sarasota resident and business partner of Ringling, acted as the primary construction manager for the mansion with Lyman Dixon and Earl Purdy employed as architectural engineers. The name of the residence, on the initial architectural plans, read "the Residence of Mrs. John Ringling." Thereafter the mansion was entitled Cà d'Zan meaning "House of John" in Venetian dialect or "House of Zany" according to Gene Plowden, indicating John's whimsy and sense of humor. *La Serenissima* or the town of Venice as it has been named, may further explain the mansions name in Venetian dialect.

Historic photograph, Gottscho, 1931

East entrance doorway

In the magazine *Country Life*, October, 1927, "A Venetian Palace in Florida" Roger Franklin Sears, with color illustrations by Norman C. Reeves, elaborates upon detailed aspects of the Ringling home.

The Gottscho-Schleisner collection of work by architectural and interior design photographers Samuel H. Gottscho (1875–1971) and William H. Schleisner (1912–1962) encompass over 285 black and white photographs taken by Gottscho of the Cà d'Zan mansion. This important documentation of the completed exterior and interior of the Ringling residence upon completion was commissioned by Dwight James Baum in February 1931. The photographs were completely obtained in 1992 by Conservation and Curatorial department staff Michelle Scalera, Deborah Walk and Ron McCarty in preparation and planning for the restoration of the Ringling mansion.

"MASS AND MATERIALS"
Historic Elements

Both the Hotel Danieli, named for Giuseppe Dal Niel, who began renting rooms in 1822 in the 14th century former *Dandolo* palace and the Bauer-Gruenwald Hotel in Venice, Italy, provided adaptations to the Ringlings' overall inspiration of the Doge Palace exterior. John Ringling's signature within the guest log archives of the Hotel Danieli clearly establishes the direct connection. Their European trips gave the Ringlings opportunity to see elaborate residences as examples of "power, wealth and hospitality" according to Dr. David Weeks quoting Mark Girouard in *Life in English Country Houses*.

Hotel Danieli

According to Dr. Weeks, the St. Bonaventure University's Chapel and Lynch Hall in Albany, New York, may have been an aspect of Mable Ringling's inspiration for the exterior designs. The cupola atop the Spanish roof tiles and terra cotta appear similar. The Chapel, the Masonic Temple and Chestnut Street Opera House entrances in New York are also possible sources of terra cotta insight for the Ringlings. In Buffalo, New York, the Blessed Trinity Roman Catholic Church built in 1924–1928 by Oakley and Schallino Architects, has columns and friezes similar to Cà d'Zan.

The site, positioning and layouts form the interior flow and functionality of this unique private residence. Dr. Weeks wrote of the finished building "Baum created in Cà d'Zan the effect of life in the grand manner on a scale that provided space without overwhelming a small company of family, friends and acquaintances. The house was designed for expansive hospitality…" Because of the circus, the Ringlings traveled extensively throughout the United States as well as Europe. This indicates their familiarity with major architectural sites throughout the country. The addition of the terrace and dock allowed for anchoring of the Ringling's yachts, gondola, and boats, all symbols of wealth. J. P. Morgan (1890–1913) owned four yachts, one, the large *Corsair,* he anchored in Venice's Grand Canal. Ringling owned three yachts, one named the *Zalophus,* Greek for sea

Zalophus

West façade: terra cotta details

Exterior decorative terra cotta details

lion, built in 1922 in Staten Island, New York, was a classic plum-stemmed cruiser he anchored along his Sarasota Bay mansion.

The prominent exterior and interior architectural features of Cà d'Zan are the remarkable façades, crafted of richly colored terra cotta ornaments. The intended visual beauty prevails in base tones of rosy, clay bisque with glazed green and blue designs. The decorative mouldings, medallions, corbels of the exterior façades and interior terra cotta decorations were created by Orman Ketcham, owner of the O. W. Ketcham Terra Cotta Works, a terra cotta firm in Crum Lynne, Pennsylvania. The Tower, 80 feet high, has a cantilevered domed ceiling and provides open air and spectacular views on all sides to Sarasota Bay and the garden landscapes. The terra cotta façades are elaborately decorated with patterned repeat motifs of leaves and acorns, owls and squirrels, cats and lions, fish and birds, and zodiac symbols. Louis XIV-style sunflowers appear throughout the eaves, Masonic imagery is on the east façade, and tall, figural male and female reliefs adorn the front entrance.

HISTORY OF CONSERVATION EFFORTS

A fter John Ringling's death in 1936, his estate was in litigation for ten years and little work was done to maintain the mansion. In 1946 the State of Florida took control of the estate. A. Everett "Chick" Austin, the Museum's first Director, moved quickly to open the mansion to the public. On December 16, 1946, over 10,000 people attended the opening of the mansion. The years had not been kind to Cà d'Zan and repairs were needed. In 1956, work was done to replace deteriorating exterior terra cotta. In 1972, air conditioning was added to the mansion, but unfortunately there was no consideration to the historic nature of the structure.

In 1980, the Ringling Museum celebrated the 50th Anniversary of the opening of the Art Museum to the public. Dr. Weeks, at that time a museum docent, was asked by the Education Department to compile information about the Ringlings from the Sarasota newspapers; later this would result in his seminal book, *Ringling: The Florida Years.*
Also in 1980, Cynthia Duval was named the first Curator of the mansion. While researching the history of the structure, Duval located Samuel H. Gottscho's photographs of the Cà d'Zan, which provided a comprehensive view of the mansion and interior furnishings. These images were commissioned by Dwight James Baum to document the mansion along with several other buildings the architect had designed in Sarasota. Duval also worked on the Historic Places nomination form for the Ralph Caples, John Ringling and Charles Ringling Estates. The Florida Review Committee for the National Register of Historic Places approved the nomination of The Caples'–Ringlings' Estates Historic District; the National designation was received in 1982. With the designation, planning began in earnest for the restoration of the mansion.

The preparations for the preservation of the deteriorating Cà d'Zan, were further encouraged when the Conservator obtained grant support from the Institute of Museum and Library Services in 1989. The grant for $40,000, a one-to one match, funded an object-by-object condition assessment of all interior furnishings, which was conducted by Marc A. Williams, Head of Furniture Conservation at the Smithsonian Institute, Washington, D.C. This initiated a campaign to fund the preservation and conservation work for both the deteriorating

architectural structures as well as the Ringlings' decorative and artistic collections. In 1989, Museum Director Dr. Laurence J. Ruggiero oversaw the 18 million dollar restoration of the Art Museum galleries and a portion of the funding was used for the exterior and west façade interior work to stabilize the mansion.

PHASED CONSTRUCTION PROJECTS

Assessment and Evaluation

In 1992, David M. Ebitz was named Director of the Ringling Museum. Working with Michelle Scalera, Chief Conservator, a plan was formulated for the restoration of the Ringling mansion. The Gottscho images of Cà d'Zan, commissioned by Baum in 1931, were critical in the preparation and planning for the restoration. In 1993, the restoration of the Cà d'Zan began with an overview assessment by Nicolas Pappas, FAIA, of Washington, D.C. Herschel Sheppard, FAIA, noted Preservation Architect from Gainesville, Florida, had also provided initial, architectural insight

specific to the launch process for funding the restoration.

George Percy, Director of the Division of Historical Resources, (DHR) Tallahassee, Florida, in 1993, strongly encouraged the Museum to initiate a Request for Proposal (RFP) Schematic Design project, a $40,000 one-to-one match grant proposal, followed by the structural restorations including the terracotta. In 1994, a projected initial Five-Year Budget and Schedule of Work for Code Corrections and Emergency Repairs of the Cà d'Zan was developed. David Ferro, Preservation Architect, DHR, was instrumental in directing and providing critical expertise. He supervised all Department of Management Services (DMS) oversight as the Ringling mansion restoration plan evolved.

The restoration work was done in three phases:

- **Phase I – 1996–1998:** Development of the Schematic Design and "Sealing the Envelope" – Major restoration, repairs or replacements of all the exterior decorative terra cotta. This proved to be an extremely complex endeavor begun in 1996, with incredibly talented artisans from Trafalgar Construction of the United Kingdom, Geoffrey Preston and Jenny Lawrence overseeing all terra cotta replacement moulds and recreations. Boston Valley Terracotta Works from New York skillfully recast all the missing and severely damaged or deteriorated elements. The major deterioration appeared to have been caused by a combination of "inherent vice" or spalling due to interior, structural support rod corrosion, rusing iron and loss, with imminent risk of urther demise to significant decoration elements overall. Recognition of this endeavor ensued with the preservation award to Trafalgar Construction restorers Preston and Lawrence and Boston Valley Terracotta owners John and Gretchen Krouse as it exemplified their remarkable collaborative restoration efforts on the Cà d'Zan extensive terracotta architectural designs. From the Belvedere Tower to the ground level terrace balustrades, the support foundations, exterior windows, doors, multi-level roof replacements and skylights were all addressed. This prepared the building for:

- **Phase II – 1998–2000:** "Mechanical Systems Overhaul" – Once the structure was "sealed" it was possible to recreate a proper environment evolved as outdated, visually intrusive electrical, plumbing, heating, ventilation, air conditioning (HVAC) systems, and ducting impeding the functionality of the Otis elevator were replaced. Asbestos abatement, upgraded security, fire, life safety, very early suppression detection alert (VESDA) systems and Americans Disability Act (ADA) code requirements inclusions provided a more comprehensive and proper environment for the Museum Collections as well as a safe and secure historic site for visitors. Computer monitoring and back-up

Belvedere Tower Stairs Terra Cotta

Belvedere Tower: pre-treatment

Post-treatment

Drawing

Mould recreation/original

During treatment

During treatment

Original/recreation moulds

Geoffrey Preston and staff of Trafalgar Construction

Original O. W. Ketcham glazed terra cotta

generators, emergency exits were all installed cognizant of the historic preservation criteria retained in all restoration projects.

- **Phase III – 2000–2002:** "Installation and Interpretation" of the mansion's furnishings based upon historical images. With new piping, ductwork and mechanical systems in place, the historic interior surfaces including: floors, walls, and ceilings were properly preserved. A series

Pre-restoration

Boston Valley Terra Cotta recreations: Belvedere Tower

Post-restoration

of investigative paint analyses, structural assessments of artistic painted surfaces, stabilization and cleaning ensued. The goal was to restore the mansion's interiors back to their original conditions. Conservation and restoration of the Ringlings' irreplaceable collections was followed by organization of collaborative teams. Both outsourced skilled professionals and the Museum's Conservation staff to perform the treatments and work.

The Restoration Project succeeded due to the numerous Department of Historical Resources grants and financial support by the State Legislature, Federal NEA (National Endowment for the Arts) grants and private foundations, corporate and individual donations.

PHASE I : DEVELOPMENT OF A SCHEMATIC DESIGN AND "SEALING THE ENVELOPE"

Restoration Architects

The first of a series of historic preservation grant awards for the Cà d'Zan restoration began in 1994 with the Florida Department of State, Division of Historical Resources. The grant request from the Historic Preservation, Grants-in-Aid category, awarded a one-to-one match totaling $80,000 to prepare a Schematic Design Plan for the Restoration of the Cà d'Zan. A grant was requested for Phase I, to fully restore all the exterior terra cotta, over 2,500 terra cotta elements overall. All preservation specific construction issues were overseen by David Ferro, Tallahassee, Florida, to follow specific directions for restoration protocol and historic building code adherence.

The second Division of Historical Resources award was for $650,000 for the preservation of the O.W. Ketcham original terra cotta exteriors, both building and terraces. David Ferro, Preservation Architect, DHR, Tallahassee, Florida, has been a constant supporter of the phased restoration projects and provided exceptional restoration expertise throughout the entire process.

The Five Year-Projected $5.8 million dollar Budget Restoration Plan, created in 1994, outlined under the then Director of the Ringling Museum, Dr. David Ebitz, evolved into a six-year-$15 million dollar project. Trafalgar Construction became Kvaerner Construction and ultimately Beers Skanska team. Alan Coombe and David Powers headed the Trafalgar team and oversaw all construction aspects of the restorations. Architect Ann Beha, Ann Beha Associates, Boston, Massachusetts worked with Beha site architect Pamela Hawkes and local Tampa architect Jan Abell. Thereafter, Linda Stevenson, Head Architect, Stevenson Architects, Bradenton, Florida provided construction renovation and restoration expertise working closely with DMS coordinator Larry Roemer.

Five Year Budget Restoration Plan, 1994

Scaffold, West Façade, Phase I

"Mass and Materials"

Historic Elements:

"*The Story of Terracotta*" by Walter Geer, published in 1896, describes the remarkable evolution of natural clays. These enduring artistic materials, once crafted, glazed, and kiln-fired become, as part of building constructions, truly architectural wonders. The O. W. Ketcham Terra Cotta Works was established in 1895 and began manufacturing its own terra cotta in 1906. It continued operations supplying materials for construction until it closed in 1995.

O. W. Ketcham studio, Crum Lynne, Pennsylvania, 1915

The National Terra Cotta Society, 230 Park Avenue, New York, New York, published an ad "The added vigor of color can best be given modern ornament by designing in terra cotta." The invention of a "Pulsichrometer," a device formulated for sprayed applications to produce a variety of colored glazes, allowed for consistency of tones and textures that were intended to aesthetically recreate the architectural effects of stone.

The location of the Ringlings' mansion, directly on Sarasota Bay, naturally exposed the edifice and all the architectural complexities to the

Classic ornament in
TERRA COTTA
lives anew because of
COLOR
available only to the
hand of the designer in
TERRA COTTA

National TERRA COTTA *Society*
230 PARK AVENUE · · NEW YORK, N. Y.

The added vigor of
COLOR
can best be given
MODERN ORNAMENT
by designing in
TERRA COTTA

NATIONAL TERRA COTTA SOCIETY
230 PARK AVENUE · · NEW YORK, N. Y.

Historic National Terra Cotta Society ads

Terra cotta "T" blocks, 1924   Southwest Terrace façade, historic view

extremes of nature: high levels of heat, constant moisture, salt air and brisk tradewinds. The "rainy season" and annual hurricane seasons posed continual threats to the overall structural integrity. Constructed of sturdy terra cotta "T" blocks with concrete and brick tiles, the inherent structural strength and the diminished risk of fire has largely prevented any major need for historic demolition. The four-story building is a blend of what has been called Venetian Gothic, with Moorish influence, Renaissance-style entrance doors and a Belvedere Tower with stunning waterfront and garden vistas.

The clay pointing, joinery, and support structure rods were adversely affected over time by harsh weather conditions. Hurricane seasons had contributed to the metal corrosion as well as the aging of the "gravina" mined marble steps on the west terrace. The marble was mined in an Alaska island quarry shut down in 1930. Over six types of diverse colored *terrazzo* marble inset tiles were utilized to create the full terrace dock and steps of the Cà d'Zan's bay view. The luminous, smooth ivory and sage green veined Mexican onyx on the decorative columns, both interior and exterior, was subject to cracking, breakage and losses.

Most of the terra cotta balustrades, with internal iron support rods, were deteriorated and actively crumbling as the brackish, or briny, salt water mixed with a cement aggregate, over time, fell victim to cumulative climate exposure and flaws inherent to the original creation.

Trafalgar Construction repaired original terra cotta ornaments and then recreated the moulds and clay models for lost originals. Historically, the modelers of the terra cotta companies were trained in Europe.

In the O. W. Ketcham factory, full-sized working drawings had to be

East Façade,
pre-treatment

created prior to the manufacturing process of the terra cotta. This incorporated calculations from architectural plans, creating working drawings and full-size detailed plans depicting layouts and measurements needed to be taken of the original pieces, clay preparations to accommodate quantities, models and mould-making. Production concerns included compression of the terra cotta clays, surface finishing, drying time, creation and applications of colors and glazes, appropriate kiln firing times of all pieces and test fittings, post firings to ensure correct alignments after firings and mass reductions in size. The models allowed for a 5–7% clay shrinkage. Some firings lasted days at a temperature of 2,000 degrees followed by cooling.

Boston Valley Terracotta cast the various clay ornamental details, matching as closely as possible, the slightly faded 1920s glazed surfaces. Inherent problems of any mould recreations include the size differentials from original to recreation due to shrinkage and adsorptions.

Boston Valley
Terracotta logo

The recast pieces: shields, medallions, cartouches, corbels, balustrades and parapets all meet the ASTM (Specifications for Architectural Terra cotta Standards) and technical data. This included fired clay bodies with glaze adhesion known as *slip* or *engobe* as applied coatings and permeability testing, shear strengths and coefficients of thermal expansion. Color matches utilized the Pantone color process and surface treatments.

Ann Beha Architects of Boston, Massachusetts, and Building Conservation Association (BCA) Terra Cotta Consultant, Ric Vierra, from New York, initiated the two year restoration.

The National Terracotta Society set standards for the periods from 1914 through 1927. Research with the Friends of Terracotta Society found variations over time as the need for higher structural standards, expansion and contraction, plus subsequent water seepage became an integral aspect of the criteria. Inherent clay porosity leads to a variety of structural deteriorations from cracking, crazing, spalling, and voids, to surface glaze loss. Maintenance and frequent professional re-pointing also known as "tuck-pointing" all areas of joinery will prevent potential, future harm. The United States Department of Interior, Office of Historic Preservation established standards required to preserve historic buildings matching color and mortar compatibility for porosity and strength. Natural environmental factors will always present challenges for possible new loss or damage. Preservation of the overall terracotta restoration is essential even though the process is massively complex and costly.

The original Cà d'Zan's 16th century red, clay Spanish roof tiles were from Granada, Spain. The new roof tiles were recreated and installed to meet the current Florida windstorm and hurricane protection criteria and building codes.

The restoration of the Court skylight was performed by Botti Studios of Chicago, Illinois. This involved the replacement of rusting or deteriorated lead based, stained glass caming and installing support structures, which addressed the constant heat, light, and annual rainy seasons on the western coast of Florida.

All exterior doors and nearly 154 windows—made of five richly colored jewel-toned French Lac or German desag, hand-blown glass—were restored or replaced. The history of glass begins with its invention by the Eqyptians, followed by the Romans, whose 1st century B.C. writer

Court skylight

Vitruvius documented the process of hand-blown fired glass, and Pozzuoli established the first manufacture of blue in Italy. The captivating reflections within the mansion's rooms, particularly the Court, are the light effects of glass tinted with cobalt, selenium, zinc, cadmium, copper, titanium, and manganese.

West Façade windows: pre-treament

Ball Construction, Sarasota, Florida, recreated the new metal window structural wood frames. Both White Stained Glass Studios, Sarasota, Florida, and Arthur Femenella, Association of Restoration Specialists of Hoboken, New Jersey, were responsible for all the lead caming, "H" rod interior supports and linseed oil treatment of the lead and zinc with auxiliary and channel caulking to prevent active water leaks from driving rains and severe storms or hurricanes.

Window treatments: in-process

Past restorations on the seven oversize doors on the west façade revealed that hundreds of aluminum strips had been utilized to accommodate a miscalculated size for the original glass opening. Sean White of White Stained Glass Studios was surprised in the disassembly of these works to discover that the aluminum post historic extensions explain both the leak ports and the glass breakage. Once properly joined and soldered, their restored durability should endure provided proper maintenance is performed by qualified professionals.

The detail oriented Ringlings cleverly accommodated the overdoor arches with inset cast bronze door surrounds, a total of fifty-two inner and outer attached artisan crafted works. Beautiful nautical motifs of seahorses, crabs, lobsters, anemones and shells, all treasured connections to the Bay upon which the mansion is sited. Restoration by the Museum Conservation staff involved cleaning, removal of surface corrosion and dirt, wax coating, and polishing to richly enhance the visual impact of these architectural works of art.

Bronze door nautical detail

Historic Terrace photograph, 1928

Recreated awnings, 1992

Awnings purportedly sewn by circus tent makers originally filtered the sunlight on the west façade; in 1992, they were recreated by United States Awning Company, Sarasota, Florida. Prior to the eventual installation of air conditioning systems within private homes, these awnings diminished the extreme Florida heat from daily, direct sunlight exposure. The mansion was a winter residence for the Ringlings who arrived in November/ December and left by March – duplicating the circus season.

PHASE II

"Ahead of its Time"

The Otis elevator, considered a major "upward mobility" innovation, was one of the first of its kind in the Ringling's private residence. First introduced publicly at the 1853 New York World's Fair, run by P. T. Barnum of circus fame, Elisha Graves Otis showcased his "safety hoist." Clearly, the Ringlings were inspired by the novelty and functionality of the elevator to access their new mansion's three upper floors in the 1920s. The company began making these new hydraulic lifts in 1878. During the restoration project, Architect Jan Abell provided critical research showing that former air-conditioning systems ductwork utilized the elevator shaft for all airflow ducting. Obviously, the elevator was rendered non-functional until the restoration removed all old ductwork and returned the Otis elevator to its' proper working order. Now, the elevator allows visitors to the upper floors. The maximum weight capacity is 462 lbs., as the historic elevator was originally made for a private, seasonal residence.

Otis Elevator ad, October 2001

19

Westinghouse stove: Kitchen

Westinghouse ad,
August 17, 1918

Pantry Room Kelvinator Refrigerator,
pre-treatment

Kelvinator ad, May 1926

Kelvinator post-treatments

Chinalain ad, May 1906

The preparatory pantry and working kitchen incorporated modern equipment such as an electric, white enameled Westinghouse Automated oven, customized as a double oven and a rather sophisticated multi-valved ceramic Vulcan cook top stove. The porcelain "Chinalain" covers on the Kelvinator electric refrigerators replaced the former style "iceboxes." Within the doors, on integral metal components, are clear signs of their authenticity by the stamped, patented inscription: Kelvinator Detroit Michigan May 15, 1923; it is also found in the Tap room's Kelvinator for chilled beverages, cocktails and a novelty known as ice cubes. A German silver sink was cleverly shaped in an "S" curve for both visual aesthetics and ease of use.

A call box, or enunciator, provided immediate staffing response from the servants' quarters to John, Mable, family and friends needs.

Crane bathroom sink fixtures from Chicago, Illinois, were included in numerous bathrooms permitting the luxury of individualized personal hygiene throughout the home.

Telegrams, rotary or "candlestick" telephones and stock ticker tape were "of the day technology" for auction contacts and Wall Street stock investor monitoring before radio and television entered into private homes. Ringling constantly monitored both his business and construction ventures utilizing telegrams from his "office at home" by frequent contact with the circus managers and his Sarasota business partner, Owen Burns.

Historic ad

Aubergine Guest Bathroom

"Inspiration and Competition"

Inspirations for the Ringling estate may very well have emerged from other American Gilded Age homes such as the Biltmore estate, Asheville North Carolina, The Newport Mansions, Newport, Rhode Island, and Hearst Castle, San Simeon, California. They were entitled "country retreat," "country estates" and "the ranch" respectively. Richard Guy Wilson, noted Architectural Historian, University of Virginia, described the Cà d'Zan as "the last of the Gilded Age mansions" to be built in America.

Ochre Court (1888–1892)
Cliff Walk, Newport, Rhode Island

Court: Mable Ringling's photograph

Court, 2006

Joseph Duveen, the *grand monsieur* behind multiple American mansions in the book *Grand Dames from 1886–1939,* was quoted "My dear woman," he told his clients, "when you are buying something priceless, no price is too high."

Italian motifs are incorporated throughout with the palace or "palazzo" using "loggias" or open, cantilevered balconies; the central "cortile" or court, the terrace or "terrazzo" the "quadrafoglio" or Ca'd'Oro, Ducal Palace of Urbino exterior façade decorations, and the stunning "belvedere" or Tower, 80 feet high.

The Tap Room originated from John Ringling's acquisition of the entire bar from Cicardi's Winter Garden, St Louis, Missouri. The artist signature "A. Brandt" is evident within the stained glass three-panel bar background and was restored by White Stained Glass.

Amon Carter is said to have given to John Ringling the bullhorns installed above the bar and, perhaps, inspired Ringling to begin the art collections for his museum, much like the Amon Carter Museum in Fort Worth, Texas. The rolled, elegant burl wood bar was fully restored by Ball Construction, involving Steven Foote and Bob Marino, both master craftsmen to preserve the stand-up bar for gents. John Ringling's private stock bourbon and period bottles of fizzy water still exist. In an Age of Prohibition, one finds the Tap Room a feisty placement within the context of 1920s era of bootlegging and boat-based "rum-runners" on the Florida coast.

Tap Room, post-treatments

Signature of stained-glass artisan

"A Time to come alive: Let's make Music"

The mansion was uniquely designed to accommodate a residential electro-magnetic musical instrument, the Aeolian Duo-Art organ, capable of playing both manually and electronically. The word Aeolian is derived from the Greek God of the Winds "Aeolus." As an integral aspect of a family tradition of music, John Ringling signed the contract for the organ on September 15, 1924, for $25,000. Today, this instrument would cost in excess of $1,000,000 to reproduce. Considered to be a forerunner of computers, avid Japanese acquisitions of electro-magnetic organs at auctions, may provide credence to this estimated value.

Manufactured as Opus #1559, the Cà d'Zan architectural plans depict all aspects of the instruments placement. Joseph Schirr, the original organ installer, signed a bottom panel board.

The carved, wood manual console is located on the south wall of the Court, with an impressive number of 2,289 lead and zinc pipes, the Great

The Aeolian Company contract agreement signed by John Ringling, 1924

Historic photo

Aeolian Company maker mark

Aeolian Duo-Art Organ, 2006

24

Choir, Swell, Solo, and Pedal sections, were installed on the mezzanine level, above the console. The Echo chamber was positioned on the second floor, the relay system on the third floor, and the motor blower was placed within a Spencer Turbine "Orgoblo" plant in the cork lined chamber in the basement. When the organ was played, the home would resonate full symphonic sound throughout the four stories, bringing an enduring, musical aura to all – family, famous friends and valued guests. The music would travel across the bay in an unforgettable, auditory memory.

The original organ plans were acquired by Conservator Scalera from the Princeton University Library after a two year search by the archivist Stephen Tinel of East Windsor, New Jersey, in 1993. Commencing with a conservation plan to return the silenced instrument back to life, multiple period instrument restoration specialists were invited to provide examination assessments. An overall breakdown of organics, deteriorated leathers, aged cotton wrapped, paraffin dipped electrical wirings, and corroded metals have prevented the instrument from playing as it was intended.

Darwin Klug, organ manufacturer and restorer, accompanied by the Museum's Conservation staff and Keeper of the Mansion, Ron McCarty, annually rotate all the original pipes. The intent is to prevent deformation of the softer metals and avoid the risk of deterioration.

The Ringlings' original architectural plans precisely accommodate every aspect of the instrument's installation in terms of construction completion. The research began in 1994 with organ specialist Nelson Barden of Boston, Massachusetts, who nominated the instrument "the organ of millionaires." At a time when an average annual income equaled about $479, roughly the price of a Model T car, the organ cost the Ringlings $25,000. Full restoration is still pending.

The Frick Mansion, the Reynolda House called the "Castle in the Sky," the Longwood Mansion and Gardens, the Marble House, and The Breakers integrated a player organ as a source of music and social entertainment of the time. As the Ringlings began entertaining, music played an essential role. Full symphonic sound was recreated within Cà d'Zan before radios and television commonly existed in private homes. E. Schinn, musical instrument expert, collaborated with Baum the architect to assure the musical functionality was precise. Over 440 original Aeolian organ rolls with 1920s seasonal, popular, classical, circus band music, operettas, and original works written and performed by great organists such as Edwin H. Lemare, are all part of the Ringling Museum's collections. Lemare had a 100–concert contract at Festival Hall, San Francisco, California for the World's Fair of 1915. Other organ rolls include Mendelssohn, Bohm, Schelling, Brahms, Rossini, Schumann,

Tosti, Ponchielli, Martin, Rheinberger, Suppe, Grieg, Herbert, Hollins, Moszkawski, Offenbach and more. Competitively, Charles A. Ringling, John's brother purchased a slightly larger, Aeolian organ in1925, Opus #1570, for his nearby home, now part of the New College campus.

The Steinway Piano from Steinway and Sons, Hamburg, Germany, is stamped within the cast iron interior 70701, with various dated components from November 29, 1859, December 14, 1869, to Ornamental Design Pat Nov 9, 1875. The piano has a beautiful wood veneer, Steinway Factory Steel Casting and a gilded, artistic instrument case.

The RCA Victrola has a mahogany wood, custom painted, gilt detailed structure and stored Ringling era player records within the cupboard.

Steinway cast/dated maker marks

Steinway Piano, Court, 2006

Historic image: Steinway Piano in Court

"Sign of the Times"

Part of the original construction, the Mansion incorporated:
- Atlas Portland cement provided the structural coatings to all of the terra cotta "T" clay brick tiles.
- Steinway Piano, New York, New York, inspired the Ringlings for a beautiful inset wood 1859 Hamburg Germany Court entertainment instrument.
- American Radiator Company, New York

Historic ads: Atlas Cement; Steinway Piano, September, 1908; and American Radiator, 1922

PHASE III

The reinstallation of the mansion was based upon the historic photographs taken by Mable Ringling with her Brownie camera during the years she lived in the mansion (the winter seasons 1926–1929), the family photo albums and the photographs taken by Samuel Gottscho in 1931.

Interior Decorative Aspects

Marble – Rich marble floor tiles of black Belgian and white Alabama marble captivate guests within the Entrance Foyer, Court and Breakfast rooms. John Ringling's Private Bathroom used

Historic Brownie camera ad

beautiful, ochre-toned Siena marble floors, walls, sink and an intriguing deep, carved bathtub. Mexican onyx, octagonal columns of a notable thickness are used throughout the Court interiors on all standing columns and are both a rare and expensive element to the design. Carved, white, marble stairwells and sloping *demi-lune* Siena marble handrails are all crafted of veined, raw ochre colored marble, materials made to be eye catching and unusual. The Court contains a carved stone mantel fireplace

The Grand Staircase   Detail, sloping Staircase

adorned with Latin inscription: *Imbre Cadente Dolce Calefieri*: Falling Rain Sweet Warmth. During the restoration, all the marble and stone was cleaned, overpaints removed, and preserved.

Woods – Pecky cypress, an indigenous Florida wood that is resistant to pests, was installed in the 40 foot Court ceiling. In the Game Room, Willy Pogany decorated interior pecky cypress wood columns and many interior doors. A "Maltese Cross" faux wood pattern in the formal Dining Room ceiling, inspired by the Palais de Justice, Rouen, France, ca.1500, were painted with stencil patterns by Robert Webb. The carved mahogany wood over doors in the Formal Dining Room have designs and wall coverings purported to have come from a deconstructed hotel. The front entrance door has a walnut exterior, intentionally aged, with a mahogany interior finish.

Asian teak floors of an unusual depth adorn the Reception room and Ballroom. These floors were restored and refinished.

Palais de Justice, Rouen, France ceiling

Formal
Dining
Room
ceiling

Tiles and terra cotta – The swimming pool on the east entrance is marble decorated with antique Spanish decorative tiles. Glazed, antique Spanish decorative floor tiles originally made for walls or fountains were incorporated within several guest bedrooms. Blues, greens, yellows with fruit and floral patterns treated guests to varietal European inspirations so prominent in the Ringlings' seasonal home.

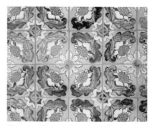

Green Guest Room tile

Gold Guest Room tile

Historic photograph: Swimming Pool

Leaded glass – The lay light or skylight directly above the Court is original to the mansion. All stained glass windows and doors were the Ringlings' desire for jewel toned colors of hand-blown, German and French Lac glass in amethyst, sapphire, emerald, garnet, and citrine, which reflect and disperse plentiful sunshine on the façades. As functional, operable doors and windows, natural wear contributes to their need for consistent care and maintenance. Any "inherent flaws" from composite silica content with alkali based minerals of glass to tempering or annealing the leaded metals cause a physical response such as fissures, breaks, or cracks. Lead and zinc as soft metals were seasoned with linseed oils and whiting and require a maintenance plan for their aesthetics and durability.

Metals – Interior wrought iron doors lead into the Breakfast Room and the nautical motif bronze doors surrounds enrich the full circle materials and techniques of artisans. Two Ringling "R" motif nine feet high window grilles are crafted of wrought iron, one recreated by Kreissle Forge, a three generation family owned and operated Sarasota business. The exterior wrought iron front door is possibly yet not affirmed to be by Samuel Yellin, Metalworker. "Yellin spoke frequently to architectural and art groups on the subject of craftsmanship," according to the biography by Jack Andrews on the Yellin foundry and historic designations from Yellin's "Job Cards."

Historic Koons photo   Bronze door surrounds: Pre/post treatments

Lighting – Many lighting fixtures and chandeliers within the mansion are creations by E. F. Caldwell. The Reynolda House's chandelier, home of owner of R. J. Reynolds Tobacco Company in Winston Salem, North Carolina, was completed in 1917 and may have provided inspiration to the Ringlings. The gold ormolu and onyx fixtures within the Court were made by E. F. Caldwell and are similar to those in The White House in Washington, D.C. Caldwell & Company, begun as a lighting and metalwork firm during the 1890s by Edward F. Caldwell and Victor F. von Lossberg, made the oversized chandeliers for St. Patrick's Cathedral and the Waldorf-Astoria. Stanford White was a friend of Caldwell. The Andrew Carnegie mansion and Taft White House, 1902, were among the earliest significant clients for the firm. Lamplighter Shop, Sarasota, Florida, with John Parker performed the rewiring of this delicate work of decorative art.

In the Formal Dining Room, sterling silver chandelier and sconces were made by Tiffany and Caldwell, as Caldwell became the foundry for Tiffany & Company. In the Venetian Breakfast room, green bead and bauble and

Waldor Astoria Court chandelier

French crystal fixture

During cleaning

Pre/post cleanings

Ron
McCarty
cleaning
crystals

Venetian chandelier
pre-treatment

Aurora Lampworks staff in
Brooklyn, New York

Dressing crystal chandelier
on site

clear crystal chandelier is from Murano, Italy. The original Waldorf-Astoria Hotel Czech glass Court chandelier, with its eighteen arms and two tiers, is attributed to European artisans from Pierpont Glassworks in New Bedford, Massachusetts. Both were skillfully restored by Aurora Lampworks, Brooklyn, New York. Higher contents of lead were permitted in Europe thus the ultimate sparkle in the clear glass crystals.

Standing torchieres in carved wood with gold leaf patterned designs illuminate the Reception room, the Ballroom and the Court on the ground floor, now fully restored.

Collections Riches

Court – Preliminary construction drawings originally planned for an open Court measuring 50 feet by 65 feet with a 30 foot high ceiling. The skylight provides a rainbow effect as the sun shines down upon the colored stained glass from above.

An enduring focal point to all who visit is the remarkable Court ceiling, painted by Robert Webb with Venetian imagery and celestial details. The ceiling was painstakingly cleaned by International Fine Arts Conservation, Atlanta, Georgia (IFACS) team of the severe water leaks and remnants of tar, adhesives and calcium deposits all were removed by cleaning with organic, non-abrasive surface cleaners and in-painted with oil pastels.

Among the collection are rare 17th century tapestries, many acquired by John and Mable on their trips to Europe. *Alexander Slaying the Lion*, 1635,

Court pecky cypress ceiling, sky light, tapestry

by Jan Leyniers and van den Hecke studios has been restored and reinstalled on the west wall of the Court. The National Endowment for the Arts awarded a $25,000 grant, requiring a one-to-one match, to the Museum's Conservation Laboratory for performed treatments by Julia Woodward Dippold, tapestry conservator, Baltimore, Maryland.

Two Louis XIV-style giltwood chairs have custom created needlepoint seats and chairbacks with delicate, *petit point* embroidery insets of Florida bird and squirrel motifs. In 1996, they were masterfully restored in the Conservation Laboratory begun with a notable Community Project by The Sarasota Chapter of the Embroiderer's Guild of America (EGA) and the Sun Stitchers Chapter of the American Needlepoint Guild (ANG) local chapters.

Louis XIV-style Giltwood Chairs

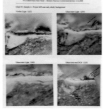

Microscopy samples

Embroiderers Guild of America
recreating Mable Ringling's chairs

Pre-treatment

Original

Recreation

Court installation

Post-treatment

Original patterns were laboriously recreated by hand-counting each and every stitch, meticulously replicating a complex grid pattern on graph paper and using a Penelope scrim base to support the embroidery. Then color matches were made from the original colors, which were largely unaffected by light, obtained on the reverse of the chair, as the front of both seats and chairbacks had drastically faded and discolored. One historic image included the chairs within the Ringling yacht *Zalophus*, which may have complicated the unfortunate, pre-restoration condition of the chairs. The chair frames were analyzed, prior to conservation, utilizing microscopy to initiate the plan for a return of the finishes back to the original appearance.

Court, 2006

Fabrics were recreated by Scalamandré for the various furniture suites within the rooms. George Allison and Alan Watkins of Designer Source, Sarasota, Florida, collaborated with Mrs. Bitter, owner of Scalamandré, to recreate special fabric patterns and designs for variety of silk, cottons and velvets throughout the mansion. Ron McCarty, Keeper of the mansion, was instrumental in connecting the original fabrics to the recreations. Wendy Cushing Trimmings of Conso Products Company provided the unique *passmenterie* and *gimp* to color match all recreated fabrics. Rubelli fabric was used to recreate the elegant patterned red Formal Dining Room curtains. The gilt bronze or *ormolu* ornaments and the purposeful retention of the historic leather on top of all three Partners Desks were respectful of John Ringling and the need to retain the original – albeit aged, leather desktop surfaces.

In August 2006, Restoration by Costikyan, New York, completed the eight month restoration process on the Napoleon III Aubusson carpet. The intended colors have been carefully preserved and the room is back to the days when the Ringlings focused their parties and social gatherings in the Court.

The Chiurazzi bronze standing torchieres were cleaned by using a finely ground walnut shell powder and the restoration process of "peening;" a low pressure (PSI) method of gently removing corrosion products and the natural, metal responses to moisture absorption. The Conservation Laboratory performed the treatments outdoors and a light wax coating was applied to preserve the patinaed surfaces.

Chiurazzi bronze torchiere   "Peening" process   Pre- and post-treatments
metal corrosion

Reception Room – *French decorative Inset paintings*
Three French 19th century decorative wall paintings with gilt frames were
removed at the onset of A. Everett Austin's tenure as the first Museum
Director from 1946–1956. Historic photographs indicate that these three
works were originally placed within the Reception Room. The works had

19th Century Decorative Inset Panels

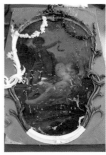

Pre-treatment   During treatment   Pre-treatment   During treatment

Inset
revealed
during
construction

Installed historically accurate   Reception Room installed original to Ringling era, 2006

35

darkened and discolored with yellowed, natural resin, varnished coatings, and multiple tears were evident overall. Cleaning of all discolored coatings, careful gap-filling of all loss areas and in-painting with alkyd paints brought the paintings back to their original artistic intent. The frame ornaments were broken and lost during years of storage, so matching casts of the mirrored image pendant pieces were skillfully recreated. The Conservation Laboratory staff conserved the works and returned them to their original location. The ultimate locations were finally determined by both historic images and the curious 54 inch wide east wall with a rather high location for the third decorative painting. The mansion's wall coverings were delicate linen fabrics almost as if fine art, painted with custom interior colors perhaps selected by Mable from her "samplings tote" she carried with her as the mansion's interior design was in process.

Three-Panel Screen – by the Jules Allard et Fils Company, with studios in Paris and New York, was skillfully restored by William Lewin and Davida Kovner. The work of art had been dismissed by some former curators until Paul Miller, Curator of The Newport Mansions, was invited to provide an expert attribution of many collection objects from the Cà d'Zan to justify conservation costs and efforts. The severe water damage from past storage

Three Panel Screen by Jules Allard et Fils

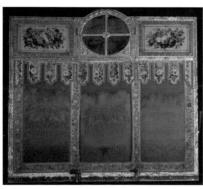

Pre-treatment

Tapestry pre-treatment detail

During treatment

Post-treatment

Historic view of Reception Room, ca. 1927   View of Reception Room, 2002

Gobelin tapestry inset detail

had adversely affected the giltwood surfaces with extensive damage evident along the base. Water absorption and subsequent structural weakening determined the restoration process, which used appropriate adhesives and resurface with *gesso*, a calcium carbonate and rabbitskin glue coating. Then, a 23.5 carat gold leaf application restored the original gilding with some distressing to match the retained original patinas. The finely woven 18th century Gobelin upholstery insets were painstakingly restored by Sharon Manitta of London, United Kingdom. Joy Abbott of The Upholstery Shoppe, Sarasota, Florida, stitched the Scalamandré recreation fabrics for placement within wood panels. The process of hand-looming has become a thing of the past, as most recently, even Scalamandré has converted to digital computer electronics looming techniques. Joseph Marie Jaquard of Lyon, France, invented a revolutionary punch card looming system in 1801 and, by 1812, there were over 11,000 operating looms in France.

Ballroom – *Dancers of the Nations*
The most prominent feature of this room is the Willy Pogany decorated ceiling, *Dancers of the Nations*. He was a Hungarian artist, set designer for the theatre, opera, cinema and book illustrator whose simple signature appears within the outermost painted border of the ceiling. Through his work for the Zeigfield Follies, the Carnegie Theatre, the "Wyntoon" Mansion, and the Hearst estate in California, "The Roaring Twenties" was

a prevalent theme. In the 1930s, Pogany became the Art Director for *The Mummy* and *Kid Millions,* Omar Kiam's Costume Designer; Busby Berkely's Production Designer for *Dames and Palmy Days;* Art Director for Fashions of 1934 with Bette Davis and Set Designer for *Dante's Inferno* in 1935. His book illustrations within *The Rime of the Ancient Mariner,* 1910; *The Light of Asia,* 1932, three diverse versions of *Rubaiyat of Omar Khayyam* from 1909 to 1942; *Wagner Trilogy,* 1911–13 with a stunning *Parsifal*

Ballroom

Condition prior to restoration

Ceiling pre-treatment

During restoration

During restoration

Near completion of regilding

Ballroom installed

image on the title page; *Alice in Wonderland, Mother Goose, Peterkin,*1940, written by his wife Elaine and *Drawing Lessons and Oil Painting Lessons* instructional books as well.

Robert Webb was quoted in a 1963 *St. Petersburg Times* article interview stating: "the ceiling of the dancing room [Ballroom] took $5,000 worth of gold leaf" in the 1920s.

As one views the decorative ceiling paintings the IFACS team worked hard to return the aged and darkened surfaces back to their original grandeur. The artist originally painted with egg tempera, casein or milk-based paints and rottenstone powder as an ageing effect traditionally used on paintings and frames. Fifty-three ceiling paintings were cleaned with solvent-blend mixtures, as they removed dust, dirt, grime, and discolored varnish. It was purported Robert Webb restored the mansions ceiling paintings from time to time and aged them by applying a dark brown substance, possibly tobacco juice.

Willy Pogany

Once the gilded octagon (polygon with eight sides or angles) framing was assessed, an executive decision was made to fully re-coat the original, wood framing with new gesso and new gilding. A small sample of the ceiling, north side of the original has been retained indicative of the pre-restoration condition. The ceiling will forever remain an icon of Pogany's whimsy and remarkable artistic skill.

Willy Pogany signature

Neo-Classical Mirrors – Two Neo-Classical carved, gilt mirrors were fully restored and properly reattributed (they had been previously considered Victorian mirrors), by the quality conservation efforts of Conservator Bernard Sellem, of The Gilded Bevel, Washington, D.C. Once the mirrors were unframed, a London, United Kingdom, newspaper dated 1896 was found within, initially supporting the Victorian (1837–1901) attribution. However, Bernard investigated and with extensive experience in period works, discovered the two framed mirrors to be authentic Neo-Classical (1660–1798).

The suite of carved gilt furniture in the Ballroom is a Louis XIV-style settee and matched chairs attributed most recently to Philippe Giubert. The recreated Scalamandré fabric modeled after a Genoese embossed velvet, and regilding of all wood surfaces were aspects of the preservation and restoration process.

Neo-Classical Mirrors

Pre-treatment   Historic view

Pre-treatment

During treatment   During treatment

Post-treatment   Ballroom installation, 2002

The Louis XIV-style gilt bronze wall sconces have a unique maker's mark unknown until they were removed for cleaning in the Conservation Laboratory – "H Vian" (Henry Vian) bronzier who specialized in light fixtures exclusively gilt bronze of the highest quality. Acquired by the Ringlings from the Astor Mansion sale, they may have been designed by Richard Morris Hunt, designer and architect. Additional "makers marks" were discovered upon disassembly of a variety of the Ringling's furniture suites, such as Turner Lord & Co., London, Kohn, St. Louis, USA; D&C, and Pierre Emmanuel Guerin or P. E.G.

Henry Vian bronze wall sconce

Formal Dining Room – The Jules Allard et Fils (1859–1945) mahogany wood formal dining room table with twenty leaves was cleaned and restored by Diego Valotti of Old World French Polishing, Venice, Florida. The original shipping crates were retained and they still have in script: *To Mrs. Ringling's Residence.* Clearly, the full table, set with all twenty leaves, would be for an elegant Court social event as the Formal Dining room is sophisticated yet moderately sized compared to other Gilded Age Mansions.

The Renaissance style, red velvet and embroidery on twenty-two chairs are some of the earliest examples of machine-made embroidery, which became popular at the end of the 19th century. The historic embroidery was carefully preserved and delicate repairs were performed by the local community chapters of EGA and ANG embroidery experts. The silk *passmenterie* and *gimp* decorative detail ornaments were laboriously recreated by Wendy Cushing Trimmings of Conso in the United Kingdom. The lush, red velvet original seat cushion covers were replaced with similar matching, special order fabric from Scalamandré.

Age deteriorated *passmenterie*, pre-treatment

Wendy Cushing recreation

Two Irish George III carved giltwood Pier Glass mirrors, circa 1755, with horizontal mirror borders were made by the John and Francis Booker brothers of Dublin, Ireland. Stanley Robertson, was a talented Conservator of gilded frames and furniture from Washington, D.C. He restored the two "broken pediment" topped mirrors and performed many repairs by skillfully applying fine quality gold leaf. Most significantly, he ascertained the proper current attribution, as the works had been previously considered simply Georgian with an unknown maker.

Formal Dining Room, 2006

The patterned ceiling of the Formal Dining room is made of plaster, cast and grained to imitate wood. The Maltese Cross design and the inset patterns painted by Robert Webb. The ceiling panels were restored by the IFACS team. Loss or damaged areas were compensated by color matched in-painting with alkyd colours. An overall protective varnish was applied for visual continuity.

Pier Glass mirror during treatment

Post-treatment

IFACS team in Formal Dining Room

Detail: ceiling during treatment

A Della Robbia workshop tondo, *Adoration of the Christ Child,* 16th century, from the Italian Renaissance period, exhibited above the carved, marble fireplace, was carefully disassembled and restored in the Museum's Conservation Laboratory. Raman Spectroscopy, a scientific analytical investigation, reveals organic pigment identification in artworks, evidenced in a spectra chart. Materials dating techniques via thermo-luminescence chromatography and petrography studies of the terra cotta clay aggregate are pending. There are three works currently exhibited as Ringling acquisitions by Della Robbia and studio. Glazed terra cotta sculptures begun by Andrea Della Robbia were intended to imitate the more expensive marble, often in outdoor environments. Curiously their family glazing formulas remain a secret. The white glazes were perhaps meant to indicate "spiritual luminosity" according to Giancarlo Gentilini. Giorgio Vasari considered the Renaissance era, 1450–1600, *terra cotta invetriata,* glazed terra cotta "a new, useful and beautiful art."

Della Robbia Tondo

Pre-treatments

During treatment   Reverse mounting technique

During treatment

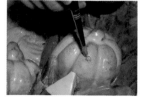

Loss recreation   Formal Dining Room installed, 2002

Foyer – The Louis XIV-style French Ormolu Coin Chest is crafted with fine marquetry, rare hardwood veneers, *ormolu* decorative mounts and a veined marble top. Old World French Polishing of Venice, Florida, restored the wood surfaces and Conservation Laboratory staff cleaned all the *ormolu* decorations. The painting by Velasquez and Mazo of *Marianna of Austria* hangs above the chest in a period-style giltwood frame precisely as the Ringlings had wanted. Two Cassone or Italian wood chests, often used to store linens, were lightly cleaned with the painted wood restored by the IFACS team.

Historic view of Foyer, ca. 1927

Foyer

Detail of Louis XIV-style French *ormolu* coin chest, post-treatment

Breakfast Room – The vaulted ceiling room with a delicate, Venetian crystal chandelier has an oversize veined marble top and carved, giltwood console table.

The suite of Renaissance Revival chairs were initially believed to be finished wood by a several former curators. Despite the Museum Conservator's intent to retain original painted surfaces, supported by scientific stratigraphy studies and microscopy analysis by James Martin of Orion Analytical Laboratories in Williamstown, Massachusetts, the decision to strip the original green painted surfaces endured. Once stripped, the five dissimilar types of woods revealed the correctness of the request to retain all green painted surfaces. A casein or milk-based paint has been used to recreate the dark earth green color with the ability to provide the slight sheen and polish desired.

Renaissance-style Venetian Chairs, Breakfast Room

Microscopy samplings

Pre-treatment

During leather preservation

During treatment

Historic view, ca. 1927

Post-treatment

Breakfast Room, 2003

All the original green leather chair coverings were cleaned and conditioned by Conservation staff and Joy Abbott skillfully reupholstered the suite of ten chairs and repaired the cushioned leather footrests. The Breakfast Room color-scheme centered on green: Venetian glass chandelier and green Venetian wood blinds.

Isabella Stewart Gardner met James Mc Neill Whistler; Mable Burton Ringling met Robert Webb and Willy Pogany. Their influences span periods from Medieval to Renaissance. Robert Webb, Jr. (1897–1986) a Williamsburg, Virginia, artist and verified apprentice/assistant to the great John Singer Sargent, often used stencils to decorate the walls and ceilings. Many of the guest room doors addressed Mable's request for a Japanese postcard design, with "hidden until opened" areas throughout the second story rooms. Webb worked at Colonial Williamsburg for twenty-three years as a superintendent of painting and decorating with Singleton P. Moorehead, a designer for the restoration department. He is also known also as a creator of the paints known as Colonial Williamsburg, (CW) paint colors.

Robert Webb, Jr.

Webb's works, commissioned by Dwight Baum, are found throughout the mansion on ceilings in the Foyer, the Formal Dining room, the Court pecky-cypress ceiling, the upper and lower mezzanine patterned decorations. A small signature on the lower mezzanine, north wall indicates his authorship.

Pecky cypress Court ceiling pre-treatment   Post-treatment

IFACS talented restoration team cleaned and meticulously restored these Webb creations, many adversely affected by time and extreme environmental conditions. From mold due to leaking roof drain pipes on the mezzanine ceilings to darkened Webb restorations and natural ageing, the paintings are now returned to their original artistic intent.

John Ringling's Bedroom

SECOND FLOOR

John Ringling's Bedroom – The thirteen-piece suite, circa 1850s, comprises a French Second Empire furniture masterpiece. The impressive mahogany and mercury gilded bronze Empire bedroom suite was crafted by one of the premier Parisian *ébénistes*, Antoine Krieger, active from 1826–1856. The original Napoleonic style suite is in the *Malmaison*, Napoleon

III and wife Josephine's palace in Paris, France. The decorative design includes cast gilt bronze winged mythological figures, crowns, putti, urns, and swags.

Diego Valotti of Old World French Polishing, Venice, Florida, performed the labor-intensive wood restorations with quality French polishing techniques. The Conservation team members, including Dave Piurek and Shay Sampson, cleaned the discolored gilt bronze or ormolu details, over 995 individual pieces, and reattached the ornament once the furniture was placed within John's bedroom. The room measures 21 feet by 35 feet with a 10 foot ceiling height.

IFACS team during restoration   John Ringling's Bedroom, 2001

The Jacob De Wit ceiling painting, *Dawn Driving away the Darkness,* 1735, was an inspiration from the former home of Alva Vanderbilt's mansion's oversize ceiling painting and Whitehall's *Crowning of Knowledge.* Both depict the same artist and similar subject matter works. The ceiling painting on canvas was restored by IFACS International, with Richard Pelter heading the team of restorers. A complete cleaning, in-painting and re-varnishing overall returned the severely darkened, discolored, and gross over-painting back to near original appearance.

Jacob De Wit ceiling painting conservation processes: 1. consolidation, 2. cleaning, 3. gap-fills, 4. in-painting and final coatings

The Louis Benjamin Marie Devouge wall painting: *Portrait of Paulina Bonaparte Borghese* signed and dated at lower right corner, 1811, was acquired by John Ringling from the Hotel Sinton–St. Nicolas in Cincinnati, Ohio. The painting was cleaned by the Museum's Conservator and serious structural tears and breaks determined the need for sensitive removal of old, linen fabric on the reverse adhered with a former glue-based lining. A new lining, utilizing a reversible conservation adhesive, Beva 371™, invented by Gustav Berger, returned the structural integrity of the painting with alkyd based in-paints on the gap-filled, former loss areas and an overall coating of non-yellowing surface varnish was applied. A new, period style-frame, recreated using Abe Munn Picture Frames, Inc., New York, mouldings, was assembled by Richard Jennings, a Sarasota framing craftsman. The French connection, with John Ringling's Napoleon style bedroom furniture suite and Napoleon's sister Paulina Borghese, depicted in the Devouge painting, coupled with the apparent similarity of Paulina to his beloved Mable, may explain the acquisition in 1916, at a then costly price of $41,000.

Louis Devouge Portrait of Paulina Bonaparte Borghese, 1811

During treatment

Pre-treatment

During treatment details

Historic postcard, ca. 1950s

John Ringling's Bedroom installed, 2002

49

The French metalworker and manufacturer Ferdinand Barbiedienne (1810–1882) crafted the impressive clock of *Sleeping Ariadne,* which the Ringlings purchased from the Henry Hilton mansion, New York. The clock was carefully disassembled and all discolored surfaces cleaned by the Museum Conservation staff. Joseph Fanelli of Fanelli Antique Timepieces, formerly of Sarasota, Florida, restored the clock to working condition and activated the captivating chime.

Sleeping Ariadne Ormolu Clock by F. Barbadienne

Pre-treatment

Post-treatment

During treatment

Detail of maker's mark

Pre-treatment

Post-cleaning

The golden striped fabrics and brocade patterned red fabrics on the twin beds, curtains, sofa and chairs are from Scalamandré.

The Stark Carpet firm masterfully recreated the precise color and pattern with the replacement rug currently in John Ringling's bedroom.

John Ringling's Bathroom – A Siena marble bathroom with a unique bathtub carved from a single marble slab and grained yellow ochre marble walls and floors glistens as an obvious luxury. Gold fixtures and a tall mirrored shaver stand complete the elegance for John Ringling's bathroom. Only minor repairs were needed to restore this room back to the original intent.

John Ringling's Siena marble bathroom sink

Exercise Room – The Koken Barber Chair from the firm in St. Louis, Missouri, was disassembled in the Conservation Lab. When Koken, now in Longwood, Florida, was contacted, they shared the fact that the striped velvet chair covering was a customized selection as leather was the dominant fabric covering for other commercial barber chairs at the time. All the nickel-plated steel was cleaned rather than resurfaced to retain the original historic intent. The wood was cleaned and refinished and the piece is exhibited upon a Florida indigenous coquina shell floor. The barber chair was a gift to John Ringling by the Czechoslovakian band known for performances at the Ringlings' home when guests were present for gatherings and social events.

Koken barber chair: damages, loss evident

Post-treatments

Mable's Bedroom – The elaborately decorated yet modestly sized room is truly unique to her taste. The furniture suite is by François Linke (1855–1946), Czechoslovakian born artist considered to be the greatest Parisian cabinetmaker of his time. The suite was first identified by Paul Miller, Curator of The Newport Mansions, Newport, Rhode Island. The exquisite Louis XV-style sandalwood with tulipwood and kingwood marquetry is adorned with whimsical swinging monkey and angel/heart motifs crafted of *ormolu* or gilt bronze decorations. Most pieces have

October 1922 cover Woman's Home Companion

purple and white veined marble tops that shimmer and shine in the natural light on the east façade of the mansion. With the recent publication of the latest François Linke, *Catalogue Raisonne,* the inherent value of all the artist's work has substantially increased according to Alton Bowman, conservator of fine French furniture. The pieces were disassembled in the

Mable Ringling's Bedroom Suite, François Linke maker

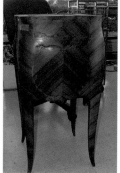

Françoise Linke Bedroom suite pre-treatment

Pre-treatment

During treatment

During treatment

During treatment

Pre-treatment *ormolu*

Post-treatment *ormolu*

Reattaching *ormolu*

Mable Ringling's Bedroom

Historic "Brownie" camera image

Detail: Tulipwood and sandalwood
with bronze *ormolu* figures/sways
post-treatment

Conservation Laboratory with cleanings performed to all the wood surfaces. The numerous ormolu pieces were detached and cleaned with *Micro-90*™, a water based cleaning product made of halogenated compounds and phenols, then well-rinsed and allowed to completely dry. A final spray coating of Acryloid B-72 methyl methacrylate varnish was applied. The individual ormolu pieces numbering over 900 parts and brass colored escutcheon pins of diverse lengths and depths were used to reattach each piece once the furniture was returned to Mable's bedroom.

The striped wallpapers of the room were hand-painted in thin colors of red, gray and green with a pale color base. The unusual, hard pan ceiling signifies the structurally supported vault area above. The decorative ceiling beams are painted with curious symbols of quotation marks, periods, exclamation points and inset wall heraldic crests. It has been suggested they were Robert Webb's humorous response to Mable's changing tastes. The IFACS team cleaned the walls and ceiling painting motifs using watercolour or Golden™ acrylic paints to retouch loss areas.

Mable's Dressing Room – Adjacent to her bedroom is Mable's dressing room and bathroom. The decorative painted cabinets and doors were designed by Webb in a Venetian inspired motif style after the Italian Baroque artist Gaspare Diziani (1689–1767). Beautiful Siena yellow ochre marble facing on an enameled white bathtub and floor complete the overall elegance. IFACS conserved the wall paintings and regilded the wood strip mouldings surrounding the cabinets. The discolored paintings and gilded surfaces had been affected by time and response to natural effects of age and wear.

Details of cabinet doors
by Robert Webb, Jr.

Image prior to restoration treatments

Palazzo Pisani-Moretta by Venetian artist
Diziani, 15th century

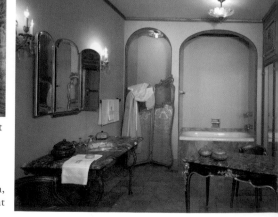

Mable Ringling's Dressing Room,
post-treatment

"MBR" Appenzell embroidery

Hand-embroidered crepe silk lace pillow covers

Mable's fine quality linens and lace embroideries were carefully cleaned by Karen Kopp and Anna Maria Troiano, talented fabric and linen embroidery experts. Some of the rarest works are on view within Mable's dressing room cabinets. Appenzell embroidery, with early inspirations dating back to 1780, is from Switzerland, and is considered to be the finest examples of 20th century linens and laces. One delicate example of Mable's collection is the Appenzell lace pillow cover with "MBR" (Mable Burton Ringling) embroidery. The richly colored set possibly mimics the stained glass window tones of four hand-embroidered silk pillow covers with monogrammed insets, are stored in the glass covered cupboard.

John and Mable Ringling's Private Loggia

Pre-restoration

Pre-restoration

Post-restoration

John and Mable Ringling's private, exterior loggia connects their East façade bedrooms. With severe, active flaking of the original ceiling painting, calcium accretions from water absorption and extensive loss areas, IFACS performed major artistic pattern recreations, consolidation repairs and in-painting to the overall painted surfaces.

Post-restoration

Guest bedrooms: *Aubergine Guest Room:* The east guest room, with a recreated Stark Carpet, Crane bathroom sink and a rare finely embroidered bed covering in delicate silk and lace restored by talented Sharon Manitta of the United Kingdom. The room was a special place for Mable's sisters and later served as the bedroom

Blue Guest Room

for John Ringling's second wife Emily Haag Buck. Mrs. Alva Vanderbilt's bedroom was lilac colored and decorated in a crème white finished furniture suite of Rococo Revival style. Furnished in the French Rococo style, Mrs. Ringling must have been astutely aware of this decorative color and furniture style theme as the guest bedroom appears to reflects this inspiration.

Gold Guest Room: the Spanish floor tiles in glazed ceramic fruit motifs with a spirited "bumble-bee" toned bathroom tiles.

Blue Guest Room: newly recreated Stark floor carpet, "Bally" fabricated in China, from an original remnant with a Venetian hand-painted bedroom suite.

Green Guest Room: Spanish glazed floor tile and white finished furniture suite.

Pink Guest Room: newly recreated Stark carpet, "Barrymore Chinchilla" fabricated in England, with a burl veneer "sleigh bed."

Pink Guest Room

THIRD FLOOR

Gameroom or Playroom – Venetian *Carnevale* scenes and imagery abound in Willy Pogany's colorful ceiling paintings with vividly real figures of John, Mable and their pets in the "L" shaped room. Dr. Weeks stated "the decorations of walls and ceiling were to represent *Fete Micareme* in Venice." The room's windows with delicate wrought iron grilles allow natural light inside to reveal the remarkable work. Pogany's imagery and details skillfully depict scenes of Venetian *doganas* and a spirited life. Pecky cypress posts with *Commedia dell'Arte* themes continue the dramatic, theatrical faces and figures from Pogany's imagination. All canvases were painted in New York and shipped to the mansion for installation.

Game Room – painted pecky cypress posts

Game Room – Willy Pogany's decorative paintings

Game Room

Detail of Willy Pogany, artist

IFACS team performed major attempts at cleaning the canvas and ultimately the decision was to carefully repaint the creme surrounds on all painted surfaces. Reattachments at weakened areas of canvas joinery were tended to with adhesives and gap-fillers then painted to match. Areas of *pentimenti* or underlying compositional changes ghosting through, indicate Pogany's various painting designs as they evolved into what is seen today.

West of the entry door, the ceiling area depicts Willy Pogany with a dog at his feet animatedly holding a paint laden brush and paint bucket, perhaps in lieu of a signature.

Fourth Floor

The fourth floor bedroom or studio suite provides views from all sides to the west Bay and the east gardens. Directly above within the room, there is a rich mahogany wood drop ceiling. Within a rare, hand-carved Venetian dressing table sits with rich and colorful birds and *decoupage* motif surfaces. Andy Compton of IFACS performed the preservation work.

Carved walnut drop-ceiling beam detail

Green Venetian blinds restored and installed

Burlington Venetian Blind Co., Burlington, Vermont, U.S.A. Maker mark evident

Fourth floor Guest Room

Lillian Alderman, skillful master stitcher of Sarasota, recreated the original window coverings throughout the entire mansion working with Ron McCarty and George Allison and Alan Watkins of Designer's Source of Sarasota, Inc. They have the unique quality of collaborating for over twenty-five years with Scalamandré fabrics. The fabrics are the Ringling's color selections abounding in brocades and velvets in rich tones of red and gold, light blue and lavender, complementing their original decorative designs. Alex Bush, VWT, installed all the recreated window coverings.

59

CÀ D'ZAN
Returned to Splendor

"Florida is a place that has lead itself well to the expression of dreams and fantasies."

Michael McDonough, Curator of Historic Buildings

In 1925 a *Sarasota Herald Tribune* editorial noted that the Cà d'Zan would be "a forerunner of scores of splendid homes, which… will grace the shoreline of our beautiful bay and magnificent Gulf." After the six years of extensive restoration, the Cà d'Zan re-opened to the public on April 28, 2002. The $15 million dollar restoration project was funded by private donations and specific, historic appropriations from the Florida State Legislature. The three major Restoration Phases repaired the structure, installed updated climate control, fire and security systems, and conserved all interior surfaces and furnishings. Through the expertise of preservation architects, structural and mechanical engineers, electrical technicians, conservators, curators and artists from around the world, the Cà d'Zan was returned to the time of John and Mable Ringling.

Michael McDonough, former curator of the Cà d'Zan, wrote that John Ringling "and many of his fellow promoters saw Sarasota as an ideal city. For the privileged few, Cà d'Zan was the magical gateway to the Mediterranean dreamland they were creating."

The restoration responsibly addressed major structural, functional and aesthetic aspects. With continued maintenance, specific, required upgrades, improved and evolving interpretations, the Ringling mansion will continue to attract enthusiastic guests. Cà d'Zan's place among America's great castles is assured by its restoration. The mansion is once again at the heart of John and Mable Ringling's vision for Sarasota in the 21st century and beyond.

Court, 2006

Floor Plan Layout

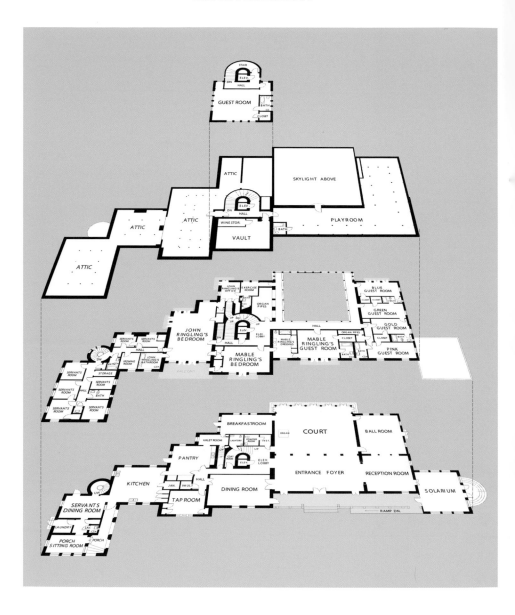

Donors to the Restoration Project

Publication:
Funded by:
Bureau of Historic Preservation, Division of Historical Resources, Florida Department of State,
assisted by the Florida Historical Commission and
Community Education Grant award
and
Michael Saunders & Co

Donor plaques:

Entrance Foyer: Linnie E. Dalbeck Foundation
Entrance Terrace: Tana and John Sandefur
Solarium: In Honor and Memory of Jean S.and Jack E.Tarr and James E.Tarr
Great Hall: In Honor and Memory of Philip and Marcia Rubin
Otis Elevator: Kenneth and Myra Monfort Charitable Foundation
Ballroom: Roy C. and Susan M. Palmer Family Charitable Foundation
Reception Room: Bank of America
Grand Staircase: Vern and Sandy Buchanan, Sarasota Ford
Aeolian Organ: Lee and Bob Peterson
Aeolian Organ Pipes: Susan Maxwell Brainerd, Ed.D., and Alan E. Quinby
Breakfast Room: William D. and Carla T. Griffin
Valet's Pantry: Tom and Gale MacCabe
Taproom: SunTrust Bank
Kitchen: William G. Selby and Marie Selby Foundation
Kitchen Pantry: Janet and Don Harvey
Dining Room: John G. and Anna Maria Troiano Foundation
Dining Room: Cary and Koni Findlay; Wendy Cushing
John Ringling's Bedroom: Ed and Elaine Keating
John Ringling's Balcony: Dr. Gene and Ruth Armstrong
John Ringling's Exercise Room: Publix Supermarkets Charities, Inc.
John Ringling's Office: David and James Allen
Mable Ringling's Bedroom: Bob and Joyce Tate
Mable Ringling's Dressing Room: Constance L. Holcomb and Walter D. Serwatka
Guest Bedroom: Goldie R. Feldman
Guest Bedroom: Betty and Marvin Danto Philanthropic Fund
Guest Bedroom: Donald G. and Joan C. Nocero
Guest Bedroom: J. Roderick and Kay Culbreath Heller
Landscaping: Founders Circle, Mable Ringling First President
Ticketing and Information: David Ebitz and Mary Ann Stankiewicz; John S. and
    James Knight Foundation; Alexander Jupin and John Bean in honor of Yuri Konrad Kruszewski

Cà d'Zan Facts

Original Building
  Architect: Dwight James Baum, NY
  Contractor: Owen Burns, Sarasota, FL
  Built: 1924 – 1926; Ringlings opened the mansion in December 1926
  Finial Cost: $1.5 million
  First opened to the public: December 16, 1946

Building Specifications:
  Exterior: Over 36,000 sq. ft (23,000 sq. ft under air conditioning); materials used terra cotta, T-bricks, and concrete
  Tower: 80 ft high
  Terrace and dock: 8,000 sq. ft. (200 ft x 40 ft) with terra cotta balustrades with tiles of variegated marble. The Bay was dredged so that it was capable of accommodating John Ringling's 125-foot yacht, the Zalophus, Mable's gondola and other boats.
  Interior: 41 rooms, 15 baths, 107 operable internal doors, 97 windows, including four floors and a lower level basement.
  1st floor: 9,200 sq. ft.; 2nd floor: 8,700 sq. ft.; 3rd floor: 2,900 sq ft. ; 4th floor: 890 sq. ft.

Restoration
Architect: Ann Beha Associates, Boston, Massachusetts (1996 – 2000), Schematic Design
Stevenson Architects (2000 – 2002), Bradenton, FL
Contractor: Trafalgar House Construction
Restored: 1993 – 2002
Restoration Cost: $15 million, which was funded by private donations and $10 million appropriation from the Florida State Legislature
Reopened to the public: April 28, 2002

COMPANIES AND PROFESSIONALS
Involved in the 1996 – 2002 Restoration

Museum Directors
David M. Ebitz, Director, 1992–2000
Arland Christ-Janer, Interim Director, 2000
John Wetenhall, Executive Director, 2000–

Finance and Administration
Walter Eisele, Associate Director 1997–2000
Lyn Bourne-Weick, Director, Finance and Administration 2001–2005

Development: Ringling Museum of Art Foundation
Susan Brainerd, Deputy Director, Development and Marketing 1993–2000
Suellen Field, now Senior Director Major Gifts 1997–

Museum Conservation Laboratory Team
Michelle Scalera, Chief Conservator 1985–
David Piurek, Conservation Assistant 1998–
Shay Sampson, Conservation Technician, 2002–2006

Curators
Mark Ormond, Deputy Director, 1994 –1998
Laurie Ossman, Riscorp Curator of Cà d'Zan, 1996–1999
Francis J. "Bill" Puig, 2000
Aaron De Groft, Chief Curator, 2001–2005
Ron McCarty, Keeper of the House, 2001–

Overview and Assessment:
Nicolas Pappas, FAIA, Historic Buildings Consultant, Richmond, VA
Herschel Sheppard, FAIA, Preservation Architect, Gainesville, FL
Florida Department of State, Bureau of Historic Preservation, George Percy, Director of the Division of Historical Resources; David Ferro, Preservation Architect

Phase I and II: Construction
Florida Department of State, Division of Historical Resources, Tallahassee, FL: George Percy, Director of Historical Resources, Bureau of Historic Preservation; David Ferro, Preservation Architect. Robert Taylor, DHR Superintendent, Tallahassee, FL

Trafalgar Construction (became Kvaerner Construction and ultimately Beers Skanska). Alan Coombe and David Powers oversaw all construction aspects of the restorations. Trafalgar Construction Geoffrey Preston and Jenny Lawrence, master terra cotta artisans; Michael Chomick, terra cotta artisan

Architect Ann Beha, Ann Beha Associates, Boston, MA: Architect Pamela Hawkes and local Architect Jan Abell (deceased) and Ric Vierra, Building Conservation Associates, BCA

Stevenson Architects, Bradenton, FL: Linda Stevenson, Head Architect; Doug Driscoll, Project manager

Larry Roemer, Florida Department of Management Services, Tallahassee, FL

John and Gretchen Krouse, The Boston Valley Terra Cotta, Orchard Park, NY

Ettore Christopher Botti; Botti Studios, Chicago, IL. Members of Stained Glass Association of America (SGAA)

Jennifer Parker, Curatorial Intern under Puig

Sean White, Kate White and Ron Estep, White Stained Glass Studios, Sarasota, FL

Arthur Femenella, Association of Restoration Specialists, Stained Glass, Hoboken, NJ

Pat Ball, Jeff Ball, Jon Pelnar and Tom Thomas of Ball Construction, Sarasota, FL

Steven Foote–custom woodworker; Bob Marino – custom woodworker

Robert Binnie–Painter, St Petersburg, FL

Windemueller Electric, Sarasota, FL

Phase III: Interior furnishings

George, Joey, Peter and Mechthild Kriessle, Kreissle Forge, Sarasota, FL

Geoffrey Steward, Head of International Fine Arts Conservation (IFACS), Atlanta, Ga. with Andy Compton, Gregory Steward, Paul Lee and Slade Tanner and Chris Hall; and Richard Pelter, President, International Fine Arts Conservation, United Kingdom with Filippo Virgili, Massimo Buschi, Michael DeCampi, and Daniel Mossi

Julia Woodward Dippold, Tapestry Conservator, Baltimore, Maryland

Sarasota Chapter of The Embroiderer's Guild of America (EGA) and the Sun Stitchers Chapter of The American Needlepoint Guild (ANG) local chapters: Supervised by: Jennifer Ashley Taylor, Project Coordinator: Marguerite Crosby, Principal stitcher: Bette Hicks and Individual stitchers include: Helen Allen, Martha Bardarik, Barbara Baxter, Jane Bell, Blanche Berry, Ellen Carlson, Phyllis Danielson, Joyce Ernst, Gladys Larson, Nanette Mathe, Joan Measer, Victoria Nessel, Karen Plater, Joan Pope, Raynore Pope, Virginia Richards, Gwen Rodgers, Katherine Schaeffer, Patricia Shulk, Dolores Steinecke, Sara Sullivan, Victoria Urban and Audry Vinarub

DMC Corporation, South Kearney, N.J. Over 35 colors and 3,000 yards of Laine Colbert, fine tapestry wool yarns donated by a generous gift from the DMC Corporation, were used to complete this task

Dawn Wilson, Gilding Conservator, Watertown, Massachusetts

Dawn Ladd, President, Aurora Lampworks, Inc., Brooklyn, NY

Paul Miller, Curator, The Newport Mansions, Newport, RI

George Allison ASID and Alan Watkins, ASID, Designer's Source of Sarasota, FL: Scalamandré; Brunschwig et Fils;Schumacher; Rubelli and Fortuny custom upholstery and fabrics

Robert F. Scalamandré Bitter and Adriana Scalamandré Bitter, FASID, owners of Scalamandré, Long Island City, NY

Geoffrey Preston and Jenny, Lawrence Trafalgar Construction, terracotta artisans

William A. Lewin and Davida Kovner, Gilt Decorative Arts & Furniture Conservators,Baltimore, MD

Sharon Manitta, Textile Conservator, Wiltshire, England

Joy Abbott, The Upholstery Shoppe, master upholsterer, Sarasota, FL

Bernard Sellem, frame and decorative gilding conservator The Gilded Bevel, Washington, D.C.

Diego Valotti, furniture Restorer of Old World French Polishing, Venice, Florida

Wendy Cushing, Wendy CushingTrimmings, London, UK

Stanley Robertson, Conservator of gilded frames and furniture from Chelsea Lane Studios, Washington, D.C.

James Martin, Conservation Scientist, Orion Analytical Laboratories, Williamstown, Massachusetts

Claudia Deschu, Objects Conservator, Bradenton, FL

Gene Mc Call, Furniture conservator, Englewood, FL

Karen Kopp, Textile professional, Sarasota, FL

Anna Maria Troiano, Textile professional, Longboat Key, FL

Richard Jennings, Gilder, Sarasota, FL

Joseph Fanelli, decorative arts, clock Restorer, Fanelli Timepieces formerly of Sarasota

Alex Bush, VWT, Sarasota curtain and blinds installation

Lillian Alderman, skillful master stitcher, Sarasota, FL recreated all the original window coverings throughout the entire mansion

James Tapley, Hand bookbinder, Sarasota, FL

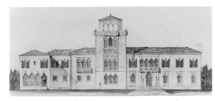 

Early watercolor drawings, ca. 1924

SELECTED BIBLIOGRAPHY

Baum, Dwight James. The Work of Dwight James Baum, Architect. Foreword by Harvey Wiley Corbett. Introduction and commentary text by Matlack Price. New York: W. Helbrun Inc., 1927.

Binney, Marcus. "Cà d'Zan, Sarasota, Florida." Country Life (October 28, 1976): 1202-1205.

Chase, Sara B. "Investigation of Interior Paint Finishes: Reception Room and Ballroom." Report prepared for The John and Mable Ringling Museum of Art, 1989.

Clarke, Gerald. "Historic Houses: Florida's Cà d'Zan: Circus Magnate John Ringling's Venetian-style Palazzo." Architectural Digest 59 (October 2002): 206-215.

De Groft, Aaron H. and David C. Weeks. Cà d'Zan: Inside the Ringling Mansion. Sarasota, FL: The John and Mable Ringling Museum of Art, 2004.

"Developing a Regional Type with a Particular Reference to the Work in Florida of Dwight James Baum." American Architect 130 (August 20, 1926): 144-148.

Duval, Cynthia. Cà d'Zan Restoration Project." Project report prepared for The John and Mable Ringling Museum of Art, 1985.

Duval, Cynthia. Historic Places Nomination Application: the Ralph Caples, John Ringling and Charles Ringling Estates, 1980.

Folsom, Merrill. Great Mansions and Their Stories. New York: Hastings House, 1963.

Frankfurter, Alfred M. "John Ringling's Greatest Show." The ARTnews 19 (1950 annual): 3-11.

Gaddis, Eugene. Magician of the Modern: Chick Austin and the Transformation of the Arts in America. New York: Alfred a Knopf, 2000.

McDonough, Michael. Cà d'Zan, the Winter Residence of John and Mable Ringling: Curatorial Report. Report prepared for The John and Mable Ringling Museum of Art, August 1989, revised August 1990.

McDonough, Michael. "Selling Sarasota: Architecture and Propaganda in a 1920s Boom Town." Department of Architectural History, University of Virginia Dissertation, 1999.

McGurk, Jonce. The Appraisal of the Contents of The John and Mable Ringling Museum and the Ringling Venetian Palace. Sarasota, Florida, 1938.

Maher, James. The Twilight of Splendor: Chronicles of the Age of American Palaces. Boston: Little, Brown and Company, 1975.

Murray, Marian and A. Everett Austin, Jr. The House that John and Mable Ringling Built: A Short Guide to the Ringling Residence. Sarasota, FL: The John and Mable Ringling Museum of Art, 1951.

Pappas, Nicholas. "Overview Assessment of the Cà d'Zan." Report prepared for The John and Mable Ringling Museum of Art, 1992.

Plowden, Gene. Those Amazing Ringlings and Their Circus. Caldwell, ID: Caxton Printers, 1967.

Sears, Roger Franklin. "A Venetian Palace in Florida." Country Life 52 (October 1927): 35-41.

Scheller, William G. Barons of Business: Their Lives and Lifestyles. Westport, CT: Hugh Lauter Levin Associates, 2002.

Thomas, Richard. John Ringling: Circus Magnate and Art Patron: A Biography, Pageant Press Inc. New York, 1960.

Tunick, Susan. Terra-cotta Skyline. New York, New York: Princeton Architectural Press, 1997.

Weeks, David C. Ringling: The Florida Years, 1911-1936. Gainesville, FL: The University Presses of Florida, 1993.

Wernick, Robert. "The Greatest Show on Earth Didn't Compare to Home." Smithsonian 12 (September 23, 1981): 62-71.

Williams, Henry Liones and Ottalie K. Williams. Great Houses of America. New York: Putnam, 1966.

Williams, Marc A. "Interior Furnishing Condition Assessment." IMLS Grant Report prepared for The John and Mable Ringling Museum of Art, 1989.

This publication has been financed in part with historic preservation grant assistance provided by the Bureau of Historic Preservation, Division of Historical Resources, Florida Department of State, assisted by the Florida Historical Commission. However the contents and opinions do not necessarily reflect the views and opinions of the Florida Department of State, nor does mention of trade names or commercial products constitute endorsement by the Florida Department of State.